Love, Laughter, and Tears

POEMS FOR ALL OF LIFE

love
laughter
and tears

POEMS FOR ALL OF LIFE

Linda Neff

Guardian BOOKS

Belleville, Ontario, Canada

Love, Laughter, and Tears

Copyright © 2003, Linda Neff

National Library of Canada Cataloguing in Publication

Neff, Linda, 1951-
    Love, laughter and tears / Linda Neff.

Poems.
ISBN 1-55306-602-2.—ISBN 1-55306-604-9 (LSI ed.)

    I. Title.

PS8577.E3347L69 2003   C811'.6   C2003-903159-4

For more information or
to order additional copies, please contact:

Linda Neff
103 Grange St.
Guelph, ON N1E 2V3
Canada
lindamaryneff@hotmail.com

Guardian Books is an imprint of *Essence Publishing,* a Christian Book Publisher dedicated to furthering the work of Christ through the written word. For more information, contact: 20 Hanna Court, Belleville, Ontario, Canada K8P 5J2

Phone: 1-800-238-6376 • Fax: (613) 962-3055

E-mail: publishing@essencegroup.com • Internet: www.essencegroup.com

In many ways, my mother, Wilma Calvert,
made this book possible.

Mom,

Thanks for your love of language, literature, and me.
So much of what I have to offer other people today comes from
what you so freely gave to me in all my yesterdays.

Table of Contents

Mirth and Milestones

Life Lessons

Preface

For my tenth birthday, my mother gave me a thick, beautifully illustrated book of poetry. She knew, even then, that poetry made my heart sing and my mind dance. Somewhere in the years since, I began to write more poetry of my own.

If life is a journey, then these poems represent places where I've paused to consider both the path and the destination. When we drive down the road and see a sign that says, "Lookout point," we should stop. If we don't, we'll still arrive where we're going, but we'll miss the view along the way.

These poems are not complicated literary pieces. They are the expressions of one ordinary woman who simply wants to know God, look at life from His perspective, and encourage others to do the same. God's love is amazing. He is always with us on the journey of real, daily life. Not only does God love us, He is the source of true laughter. After all, He created baboons and penguins, didn't He? He loves, He laughs, and He also weeps. When Jesus came to the tomb of His friend Lazarus, and saw his family grieving, He wept. "The Lord is close to the brokenhearted" (Psalm 34:18a).

Love, laughter, and tears. A lot of life is summed up in those three words and echoed in these poems. Some of the poems have explanations. Others I have chosen to leave "blank." My prayer is that whatever you, or someone you love, is experiencing right now, these poems may encourage you to see God in all of life. He is there.

No book, of course, is a solo effort: my deepest thanks to Mary Fisher for volunteering to do the computer work. Your loyal friendship is one of my life's best treasures.

Much gratitude goes to George and Heather Farnworth and my daughter Julie Neff for their enthusiasm and help with this project. Helen Miller, my prayer partner, has shared much love, laughter, and tears with me during the past few years. Thanks again.

My husband, Dave, while he does not love *poetry*, does love *me* very much. This means more than words can say.

Finally, my special thanks goes to the friends and family who have allowed me to be part of their celebrations and struggles. By sharing your lives with me, you have blessed me beyond measure. You are loved.

Because of God's amazing grace,

Linda Neff

Love and Friendship

Tea, With Love

We sat for tea,
The sun streamed in,
We wept.
She felt so frail, inept,
And for my part,
In some small way,
I understood.
And it was good
To know that God is using last year's pain,
For this year's listening.

That's how it is in kingdom-life:
The hurts I think will never end
Soon mend,
And teach me how to be a friend.

Something Special
for His Kingdom

The woman at the well,*
He knew her well,
She knew Him not,
He drew her in;
Her lot
In life was scattered.

Men wanted her,
But loved her not.
To Jesus Christ she mattered
In a different way.
She didn't understand at first,
When she dropped down her jar
To give Him water for His thirst.
He loved her at her worst.

A miracle for sure,
A drink of living water pure.
It made her clean,
It made her whole,
It satisfied her soul.
It made her life
Mean something special
For His kingdom.

Written for a friend who regrets her past. She has been a great blessing to our family, and many other people.
*see John 4:1-42.

My "Aunt" Ivey

Though many people
Touch our lives
In wonderful ways,
Coloring our days
With special hues,
Only a precious few
Are always there.
Like loyal, lifelong cheerleaders,
They applaud and encourage,
Taking joyful intense interest
In all our moments,
Both gain and pain,
From birth to school to career,
To marriage and motherhood.
"Aunt" Ivey was one of these
Precious few
For me.

And how I loved her for it!
Selfishly, perhaps,
Enjoying her loyal love.

Still, I am richer,
And I hope, better
At loving others
Because of her example.

Memories of her hugs,
Her teaching, her laughter,
And many meals and times together,
Form bright threads
In the fabric
Of my life's tapestry,
And I will not forget.

Written at the time of Ivey Snoddy's death, with gratitude to her daughter, Marnie Wilson, for sharing her wonderful mother with our family.

Dr. Keith Price

There once was a man called to preach,
And his life was no day at the beach,
It meant study and working,
Preparation—no shirking,
But God gave him such great Truth to teach.

In the summer of 1999, I had the privilege of hearing Dr. Price speak at Fairhavens. This little limerick was my way of saying thanks. Such a dear, great, godly man who went home to heaven in October 2000.

When and Then

When we kneel together at His cross,
The ground is level.

When we weep together at His feet,
The tears are mingled.

When we suffer together at His side,
The pain is eased.

When we pray together in His presence,
Our God is pleased.

When He heals our wounds,
Our scars have value.

When He lifts our heads,
Our faces humbly shine.

When He smiles at us,
We hear Him say, "You're Mine!"

And then we walk in freedom,
As He leads us.

And then we lead our fellow pilgrims
With God's love.

And then we minister the life of Jesus,
Flowing through us.

And then—the Lamb, the Lamb, for always,
And then—the El Shaddai forevermore,
And then—the Mighty One, in all our days,
And then—His mercy, more and more.

Threads

Threads of friendship,
Start with three:
God and you and finally, me.
Braided together,
With laughter and tears,
But through the years,
There were gaps that we missed,
But this lapse could not pull
Threads apart,
For our hears were so full,
When we met once again,
There were more threads to weave,
Special ones, I believe,
Made from life's love and loss,
Marked with gold, by a Cross.

And our thanks to the One,
Who makes friendship so fun!

Bloom Where You Are Planted

Bloom where you are planted,
Shine where you are sent,
Know that God has used you here,
Just the way He meant.

Love where you are living,
Serve where it's His will,
Know that God has plans for you,
Only He can fill.

Grow where you are going,
Weep when you're in pain,
Know that God restores your soul,
Makes you whole again.

Pray when you are breathing,
Laugh when you exhale,
Know that God is near you,
Never will He fail.

Cherish all the memories,
Make a brand new start,
Know that God has placed you all,
Forever in our hearts.

Written for friends who moved to another place of ministry.

For a Little Friend, As She Grows Up

I see you soon,
Full of God's grace,
Joy on your face,
Finding His place,
For you, in life,
Using the gifts He's given you,
To bless the world you live in.

I see you still—so many memories,
I see you soon—so many prayers,
I love you lots—and hope to see you again soon.

My prayers for you
Are like cocoons,
Hopes gathered snugly,
Quietly.

Patient waiting time,
   The answers will be…
      Like butterflies,
         Emerging slowly,
            With beauty.

Grief and Suffering

Beauty in the Beast

Pain is a beast,
When we expect it least,
It roars,
And makes us cringe
With fear.

Its repulsiveness
Makes us want to turn
Or run the other way.
Pain is a beast,
Clothed in ugliness.
Turning, or running,
Or screaming in its face
Leaves us dead, while it lives on.

But beauty,
Reaching out with love and faith,
Makes a miracle.
The mask of ugliness pain wore
Drops away.
We see what God saw all along:
The Prince of Peace,
Revealed to us through pain.

*Written for a friend, who suffered the "beast" of abuse, and now lives
a life of beauty and compassionate usefulness to other people.*

Tears

Tears of sorrow,
Tears of grief,
Hope for tomorrow,
Tears of relief,
Tears of pain,
Peace comes after
Drought, like rain,
Tears of love,
Tears of grace,
Flowing in a new direction,
Pain is a watershed place.

Stained Glass

Sometimes the pieces of our dreams,
Like bits of colored glass,
Lie broken all around
On the ground
Of dark reality.

All our efforts
To fit the fragments
Back together
Fail.

The Master Designer
Scoops them up,
Forms a fresh pattern,
Frames it with His strong love,
And lets His own warm light
Shine through the broken shards,
Creating a color-dance of hope.

 For Now

This is your life, dear one, for now:
The confines of a room, a chair.
Disease endows
A body bound, and there
You stay, day after day.

This is your life, dear one, for now,
A painful chance to trust God's grace
A husband who will keep his vow,
As both of you just seek God's face,
Day after day.

This is your life, dear one, for now,
Blessed with a conscience clear, for faithful duties done,
And memories that a mind and heart allow,
Still victories to be won,
And prayers to pray, day after day.

This is your life, dear one, for now,
Before our mighty, loving God,
The confines of your room must bow,
To One whose staff and rod
Can comfort you day after day.

This is your life, dear one, for now,
Yet there are many who still call you friend,
And wonder why this suffering God allows,

And pray that you will mend,
Day after day.

This is your life, dear one, for now,
Your pebble drops in water,
Causing circles wide and lovely—how
God makes your life to matter,
Loving ripples sent, day after day.

Losses

What can I say?
I've never lost a child,
But I've had other deaths,
And losses that brought pain:
Dreams conceived in hope,
And dashed on the rocks of reality,
Hopes blown away
By the winds of change,
Feeling helpless,
Knowing others do not understand,
But knowing
Jesus understands and loves,
For He had pain and sorrow, too.

The Legacy

A legacy is left today
Which cannot be regarded in the usual way:
Divided, counted, used, and banked.
This treasure that is left
Is one for which our God is thanked.

And though his family grieves
His loss, and feels bereft,
Still precious is the knowing
That their loved one's faith was growing,
And a living legacy he leaves,
More lasting than mere things:
The faith and hope and love
He found in Jesus, King of Kings.

Song of Ruth

Sing of quiet faithfulness,
Sing of steady love,
Sing of gentle loveliness,
Sing of God's great love.

Sing of two score years and ten,
Sing of family ties,
Sing of earthly journey done,
Sing of sad goodbyes.

Sing of all that's gone before,
Sing of memories sweet,
Sing of God's great grace and more,
Sing of saints to meet.

Sing of earthly dreams not done,
Sing of hopes and fears,
Sing of final victory won,
Sing of joy, with tears.

Sing of God's surpassing peace,
Sing of hope, with pain,
Sing of God's Lamb sacrifice,
Sing of Jesus slain.

Sing of Christ who conquered death,
Sing of sin's price paid,

Sing of a place in heaven,
Sing of mansions made.

Written for Ruth Ferris, who died in March, 1999. Victor McQuade composed a lovely tune for this poem, and The Grace Community Church Singers sang it at her funeral. Ruth was a woman who loved her family and her God, and faced forever with confidence.

God's Lap

Dear God, I was too glib,
My answers were too pat,
For where she's at.
I should have told her
You would hold her
If she'd crawl into your lap,
Lean her head, in quietness,*
On your strong shoulder.

I was too quick to say, "Cheer up."
I did not wait
For needed tears to fall.
You do not mind at all;
You gather weeping drops into a bottle,**
Saved as a reminder of Your care.
Your heart and lap are large,
And we are small.

*see Psalm 131.
**see Psalm 56:8 (KJV).

These Three Remain

A loss
Still leaves
An empty place,
Bordered by bittersweet
And tears,
For all the years
Of struggle.

Still hope remains,
That God has gathered her
To Himself,
As He will do for you,
As you grieve
And believe
That for some struggling ones
Death comes
With healing and with freedom,
When life's span did not.

So—jubilation!
That faith remains
In One Who watches
With tenderness
The sparrow fall,*
And over a multitude of sins
Covers all
With love.**

Written for a friend whose mother died believing in God, but still battling alcoholism.
*see Matthew 10:29. **see I Peter 4:8.

The Gift and the Legacy

There is no gift like someone
Who loved his family.
There is no gift like someone
Who lived a legacy.

A legacy of service
To people of all kinds,
A legacy of faith and hope
Impressed on hearts and minds.

A legacy of laughter,
Of games and fun and play,
A legacy of knowing God
Gives joy to each new day.

A legacy of friendship,
Both new and through the years,
A legacy of listening
To people's hurts and fears.

A legacy of worship
To Jesus Christ his King,
A legacy of peace and love,
That only Christ can bring.

There is no gift like Jesus,
Who loves God's family,

There is no gift like Jesus,
He is our legacy.

Written for the family of Dr. Hany Rafla, at the time of his death, July, 2000. He was a wonderful physician, loving husband, father, son, brother, and friend.

Hello, Again

You did not get to say "Goodbye."
You wanted to,
And this is why:

You loved him so.
But this you know:
When you die too—
(And you will someday),
You'll get to say
"Hello" to him,
Again, forever.

Sent to friends when their Christian teenage son died suddenly.

Dusk

Night is falling,
God is calling,
Sunlight disappears.

Shadows deepen,
Feelings keep in
Concert with our fears.

Hearts are crying
Wondering why and
How and what and when.

Answers fade out,
Questions bring doubt,
Hope will come again.

Dusk is like a velvet shawl,
Given by God to wrap us all,
Golden light's gone from the sky,
Lord, we lift your Name on high,
Grant our weary souls rest,
In your shawl of peace we're dressed.

For a friend, whose suffering seemed harder at dusk.

The Rope

I cannot say I know
Exactly how you feel,
For I have never faced
What you do now.

But I have had
Bleak days when joys and hopes,
Once bright, were then erased,
And I was left wondering "why" and "how."

Why me at all,
And why me, now?
How can I cope,
And who will hear me when I call?

Someone has said, when hope is gone,
And we are at the end of our life's rope
That we should tie a knot,
And just hang on.

I think that how we cope
Is like a rope,
Made up of intertwining strands,
We hold these in our hands:

Friends' love,
Doctor's skill,

Around, above,
Beauty still.

Yet there is more—
The strand that is the strongest, yet most fragile,
Forms the core:
It's called perspective.

Perspective is the eyesight
Of the heart and mind we choose,
That helps us see what others miss,
The loveliest of news, it's this:
That at the end of our small rope,
When we don't know what else to do,
Jesus is there, too.

He is There

When you do not feel
Courageous or confident,
Spiritual or joyful,
He is there.

When your heart is breaking,
And your emotions aching,
He is there,
And He is making you more like Jesus.

When there are decisions to be made,
Groceries and gas to be bought,
Yet everything in you cries
For life's mundane details to stop,
Stand still,
So you can collect yourself,
He is there.

When all your questions
And answers
Seem to dangle in mid-air,
He is there.

Who is He?
Who is this One?

The Alpha and the Omega,
The Beginning and the End,
El Shaddai,
The God Who is there,
For you,
Now.

For friends, when they found out that their young son had cancer.

Irreplaceable

Mothers are irreplaceable,
But memories remain.
Sorrow is a crucible,
Used by God, again,
For the refining of our hearts
And minds, for wider service, still.
He helps us through the painful parts,
He can, He does, He will!

Written for a friend when her mother died.

The Tributary

The love of God,
Like a river,
Flows through our lives
To others.
Each "other" is like
A separate tributary,
For that one only.
So though love's river
May have many branches,
The death of one
Still leaves us with a cut-off feeling,
For the flow of our caring
Has nowhere to go
But memories.

God bless your memories. And may the severed place in
your heart become a garden.

Written for a friend, when her father died.
I think it was C. S. Lewis who first introduced me to the concept that our
love for each person is like a tributary. No matter how many people we
are privileged to love, the "numbers" do not make up for the loss of "one."

Love and Nailprints

How honored I am
When someone is honest,
And shares the hard times she is facing.

So, you have honored me—
Thank-you!

Your family finds a special place
In my prayers,
Because I believe
In the One
Who Himself experienced
Rejection and brokenness.

He reaches out to help
With hope and healing.

The nailprints in His hands
Match the love in His eyes.

Account Full

Some fathers leave
Land and house,
Money and things,
Stocks and bonds.

But, oh, the riches and the wealth
A godly life leaves
To those who remain.

So, in the pain
Of loss and longing
For more earthly times together,
Still you draw on the account
Your father left full:
A life well-lived,
Given to God, His Truth, and people.
A wealth that will not
Rot, or
Rust, or
Wear out, or
Be stolen by thieves*
Ever.

We do not grieve as those who have no hope,**
Yet we do grieve,
And the empty, hollow places
Left by your father's passing

Are filled by the One Who said:
"Blessed are those who mourn,"***
And also by the thrilling certainty
That your father's life
Was well-lived for eternity.

*see Matthew 6:19-21.
**see I Thessalonians 4:13.
*** Matthew 5:4.

Intruder

Pain never knocks,
Nor does it ask permission.
It barges in life's door,
Uninvited and unwanted.

While we ask "Why?"
Pain steals away our strength
And saps joy dry.

But soon we find
That pain leaves gifts behind.
The theft of what we cherish
Clears away the clutter,
So we discover:

Faith—that tangled problems
Will unravel and smooth out someday.
Hope—that healing will allow us
To help others as we are being helped today.
Love—that sees the beauty of committed caring
Through tough times,
And finds that "whole"
Is not a quality
Of body,
But of soul.

Written for a friend, who lost part of his hand in an accident.

Mirth and Milestones

Signposts

Age, a birthday,
Is only a marker,
A signpost
Of the coming and the going
Of what we value.
The world dreads
Seeing the signposts
Because all that it values
Is going,
Not coming.
We who know God,
Know that our physical bodies
Are going,
And Jesus is coming.

Hallelujah on our birthdays!

"The outward man does indeed suffer wear and tear, but every day the inward man receives fresh strength… for we are looking all the time not at the visible things, but at the invisible. The visible things are transitory; it is the invisible things that are really permanent" (II Corinthians 4, Phillips New Testament).

"The world and all its passionate desires will one day disappear. But the man who is following God's will is part of the permanent, and cannot die" (I John 2, Phillips New Testament).

Another Year

Another year...
More laughter,
　　More love,
　　　　More gifts
　　　　　　From above.
　　　　　　　　More learning,
　　　　　　　　　More pain,
　　　　　　　　　　More growing,
　　　　　　　　　　　More gain,
　　　　　　　　　　　　More to see,
　　　　　　　　　　　　　More to hear,
　　　　　　　　　　　　　More to be,
　　　　　　　　　　　　　　This year
　　　　　　　　　　　　　　Like Jesus.

The Servant

The King of all the earth,
Knelt down to wash His followers' feet.
He said, "You will be blessed if you do likewise."*

And he does, this servant of the King.
He notices another's need,
And helps with quiet, loving deeds.
These acts of help
Are like a patchwork pattern
Of God's grace and call,
A living quilt of caring
That wraps around us all.

Written for my wonderful father-in-law, Ronald Neff, on the occasion of his 75th birthday.
**see John 13:17.*

Gifted Hands

Her gifted hands
Carefully craft so many pieces,
Selecting colors, patterns, styles,
Keeping the final lovely picture in mind.

His gifted hands
Carefully craft the details of her life,
The Master Designer chooses as He wills,
Her parentage, stature, and skills,
Making a unique pattern and style.
All the while with love He weaves
The colored threads
And leaves nothing to chance:
Yellow for joy, red for redemption,
Green for growth, blue for blessing others,
And the black outline of suffering
That brings out the beauty of all other hues.

God's gifted hands work and choose,
Keeping in mind the final perfect picture of His Son,
For when Christ appears, she shall be like Him,
For she shall see Him as He is.*

*Written for my lovely mother-in-law, Gladys Neff, on the occasion of
her 75th birthday.*
*I John 3:2.

Only Yesterday

Only yesterday, it seems,
We traced the outline
Of your tiny newborn hands,
So new from heaven's heart,
Fresh-scrubbed, bright-eyed,
Gift-wrapped from God to us.
And we, in turn,
Gave what we had for you:
Clothes and food and shelter.
Even then we knew,
Jesus was there too.

Only today,
Light-years away,
Chickenpox, and skipping ropes,
Sandboxes and tricycles
Are memories we trace
As you stand tall tonight,
Fresh-scrubbed in graduation clothes.
Even now we know,
Jesus will be with you as you go.

Only tomorrow, and the next day, and the next,
Line up like question marks
To which only God knows the answers:
Shadows of sorrow, light beams of joy,
Rainbows and rain, laughter and pain.

So with the eyesight of your heart
Trace the outline of His grace,
In each of life's events,
As we have traced His handiwork
In making you.

All we have to offer you is Jesus,
And Jesus will be all you ever need,
So lift your heart to Him
And let Him lead.
Strength when you are weary,
Joy when sadness fills your soul,
Peace when storms and trials come,
Wisdom to pursue a righteous goal.

For our daughters, Sarah and Katherine Neff, Crestwicke Academy Graduation, 1996.

One Symphony

Starting with a single note,
The music grows,
And flows
From one life
To another.
Friendships come and go,
But one remains
To make the music of a marriage.
Discordant notes of selfishness
Take time to temper.
Slowly, sometimes painfully,
The songs of two hearts
Become one symphony,
Starting, blending, ending,
With a single note
Of Grace.

Written for a musician friend at the time of his wedding.

Ode to the Anniversary Couple

Awards hang on walls,
Gathering dust,
And rust can rot
The best of our inventions.

Worldly fame can fade
With the fickle whims
Of human attention.

Wealth can walk with misery,
And not buy faith, or hope,
Or persevering love.

Twenty-five years of marriage—
Now, there's an achievement
That lasts,
And pleases God,
Giving children
Parents to be proud of,
Who help them see
That love is daily,
Does not give up,
A race run by Grace.

You Are Two With Grace

There are those who say they're faithful,
Yet there are those who live it out,
There are those who break their promise,
Yet there are those who leave no doubt.

You are two with perseverance,
You are two who've known real pain,
You are two with strong commitment,
You are two with life-long gain.

There are those who quit their loving,
Yet there are those who humbly seek,
There are those who dig their heels in,
Yet there are those who will be meek.

You are two we are so proud of,
You are two we love so much,
You are two with grace to speak of
You are two who've known God's touch.

Prescription for Retirement

Take away the stethoscope,
Never wonder how you'll cope,
Add in travel time, and then
Wonder how you ever worked—and when?

Consequences will be dire,
If you do not now retire,
Give your heart and mind a rest,
It will turn out for the best.

Sitting in your easy chair,
Keeping out of your wife's hair,
Remembering dispensing drugs,
Is not as fun as swatting bugs.

Leaving years of your career,
Appreciation you should hear,
But the best is sometimes last,
Laugh, and love, and have a blast.

Friends and family still are yours,
God will open up new doors.

Written for a friend on his retirement after more than forty years in family medicine.

The Five Senses of Leadership

To lead
Means many things:

A sense of need
For the grace God brings.

A sense of vision, seeing
Far beyond today
To future times, and being
Mindful of God's ways

A sense of kindness
Knowing that each one
Has hurts and blindness,
Battles to be won.

A sense of humor, laughter,
Lifting hearts and brightening faces,
Troubles seem much smaller after
Humor puts them in their places.

A sense of wisdom, insight,
Yours for fearing God, not man,
Courage just to do what's right,
For your work is in God's plan.

For a friend, who took on a new position of Christian leadership.

My PMS Lament

I'm mystified and I'm mortified,
And most of the time, I'm fit to be tied.
I feel jumpy and jittery and downright crabby,
And, worst of all, I can be quite gabby.
My memory of failures gets better and better,
Right down to the very last painful letter.
I carefully go over all my past hurts,
My energy level's in fits and spurts.
Nothing I do ever seems quite right,
From early morning, to late at night.
I spill the juice and drop the butter,
And those nearby can hear me mutter:
"Bear with me please, if you can, if you will,
For in seven short days, I'll be an angel."

Menopause Muse

Only yesterday it seems,
I went from carefree, childhood days
To all the monthly moods of teens,
And other adolescent ways.

Where did the intervening decades go?
When pregnancy and giving birth
Went by so fast—I want to know
If ending this, I still have worth.

I visited a store one day, all red,
The clerk asked me if I was well,
I knew it was a hot flash, so I said,
"I'm fine." I could not bear to tell

This woman, whom I hardly knew,
That menopause was stalking me,
And daily my depression grew,
I wondered when I would be free

To figure out just who I was
At this prime time of life, the final half;
I'm now a menopausal woman, does
This mean that at my symptoms I can laugh?

You bet I can. There is enough material here
To fill a stage with stand-up comics,
But if they are young and male I fear
The menopausal women might throw bricks!

My Cat's Life

Sometimes I wish
To live the life my cat does:
His decisions are
Limited in complexity,
Glorious in simplicity;
His responsibilities are
Glaring in their scarcity,
And fun in their felicity.

He thinks: "Shall I sleep now,
Or gaze outside, and ponder
By the window pane,
How long the rain
Will keep me in?
Today, perhaps, I'll want to play,
Chase butterflies and birds,
I have no words
To play with, only paws.

But back to sleeping—
In keeping with my need
For frequent naps,
Perhaps the energy it takes
To find the perfect bed
Just makes me tired,
So many choices, so much time.
I choose a sunny spot on a soft couch,

Although a corner by the stove still beckons,
No one reckons how the stress of this dilemma,
Causes me to shed my fur each day, all year.

Oh, dear, just as my eyelids close,
My favorite sound awakens me:
Hum of can opener on can,
The drumbeat of the spoon on dish."

Like I said,
Sometimes I wish
I lived the life my cat does.

The Saga of Sammy Lee

Now a fisherman named Sammy Lee,
Had been fishing for most of his life,
When he wasn't trawling the blue-green sea,
He relaxed at home with his wife.

While dozing there in his favorite chair,
He would dream, when the day was done,
Of the time he would catch and fling through the air
A shimmering fish called "The Big One."

He told his dream to some other men,
Who fished in the blue-green sea,
They said they shared the exact same yen,
So they challenged Sammy Lee.

The date was set for Wednesday next,
At dawn, come rain or shine,
An impartial judge was chosen,
To weigh what they caught from the brine.

Sammy Lee and the other men,
All met, when the big day came,
Each one with rod and reel in hand,
Face set to defend his name.

The sea was calm as the boats set out,
To find the biggest fish,

Each man had chosen his favorite bait,
To fulfill his fondest wish.

Sammy Lee snagged something strong,
That pulled his line long and hard,
But when he lifted out the hook
It was garbage he had to discard.

He finally did catch a very big fish,
And landed it safe in his boat,
But he put in his line to try once again,
'Cause he wanted to win and to gloat.

At the end of the day, the men came to shore,
In their boats, with tales to tell,
Of "The Big One" sighted, and almost caught,
But escaped in the blue-green swell.

The judge stood there on the dock with the scales,
While the fisherman watched and whined,
He weighed each fish and decided to say,
"Now men, this is what I find:

I've checked the size of each slippery one,
You have brought to me this day,
But the fish that weighs by far the most,
Is the one that got away."

*Written for my son, Eric Neff, who loves to fish. And for my late
father, William Calvert, an avid fisherman, who would have loved Eric,
and would have enjoyed taking him fishing.*

Life Lessons

Bypassed

It happened again—
Bypassed for an opportunity
That I really wanted,
I felt hurt, resentful.
Flitting thoughts of frustration
Pecked at the edges of my mind.
Annoyed at their presence,
I flicked them away,
And turned my thoughts to God,
Confessed my pride, and selfishness,
Reviewed His awesome ability
To orchestrate the events and opportunities
Of my life.

Promotion does not come
From east or west,
But from my God,
Who knows what's best.*

Lord, in still, small voice,
You said to me,
"This is a test,
To prove you know
How to trust Me
When you hurt."

Yes, Lord,
Now *this* is an opportunity

To honor You,
That I would not
Ever
Want to bypass.

see Psalm 75:6,7.

Changepoints

Changepoints—those pressure points
Where expectations and uncertainty
Merge and converge,
Until we kiss our comfort zones
Goodbye.

Questions—our own and others'
Probe and prod and goad,
And leave us shaken and confused.

What am I going to do?
Where am I going to be?
Why, and when, and how, and who?
The future of me!

Answers—we want them
Neatly packaged, delivered to our door,
And more—let them be fun and easy:
Roller coaster living makes us queasy!

May all your changepoints be anchored
In the One Who does not change.

Written for a friend "in transition." With thanks to Joyce Landorf for the word "changepoints." Many years ago, she wrote a book by that title.

Women of the Kingdom

For such a time as this,
An age, a day, and hour,
When world events and people's lives
Need touching by God's power.

For such a time as this,
When all around they say:
"Where's God to come and heal and help?"
People, people are His way.

For such at time as this,
He wants to use our hearts
And hands, our eyes and ears and feet,
To take an active part.

For such a time as this,
Queen Esther stood near death,*
To bravely keep her people from destruction
Though it cost her breath.

For such a time as this,
God wants a woman strong,
Like Esther, facing violence and hate,
Meeting these wrongs.

For such a time as this,
The world has yet to see,

And hear what God can do with women,
Who will humbly bow their knees,
For such a time as this.

Written at a Navigator women's conference, Glen Eyrie, Colorado, 1985. With gratitude to all my prayerful, loving, spiritual mentors who serve with the Navigators.
*see Esther 4:14.

Simon Peter

Simon sweated
That hot day
In Galilee.

When he dreamed
Of the future,
There only seemed
An endless dance
Of days and nights,
Fishing, mending nets,
Bone tired,
Nothing certain,
Nothing sure,
Least of all,
His own feelings,
Up and down,
Easily erupting
Like those waves
And storms at sea.

Then one day,
Jesus of Nazareth
Looked at him,
Steadily, lovingly,
And said something
Miraculous:
"Your new name,

Your new identity,
Is 'The Rock'."*
Stable,
Sure,
Calm,
Certain.

*see Matthew 16:16-18.

The Mercy Group

Left out?
We long to be included
In a group of special people.
On the outside, looking in,
Like kids at the candy store,
Noses pressed to the window.
I've felt that pressure on my nose!

What is the ultimate "in" group?
God has His own.
We are in it by His mercy.

And someday, safe in God's arms,
We'll look across the chasm*
That separates heaven and hell
At those, many of whom are "in" now,
And then will be "out"
In everlasting darkness.

And the fleeting feelings
Of being "out"
That we may experience now
Will never match
The eternal pain they'll feel then.
Let's love them,
And tell them

About the Mercy Group
While they still have
A chance to join.

see Luke 16:19-31.

Frumpy and Fabulous

Here I sit,
Watching them walk by
In designer jeans, and fur jackets,
And real leather everything.

Frankly, I feel frumpy,
Homely,
Unimportant.

Thankfully,
I carry with me
A copy
Of the King's book.
In it I read:

"But you are a chosen people, a royal priesthood, a holy nation, a people belonging to God, that you may declare the praises of Him Who called you out of darkness into His wonderful light. Once you were not a people, but now you are the people of God; once you had not received mercy, but now you have received mercy." (I Peter 2:9,10)

Written in a hotel lobby, Houston, Texas, December 1983.

The Waiting Room

The waiting room
Chairs seem uncomfortable,
The view outside seems
Dull and cloudy.
The Great Physician
Seems to be attending
To other people.
Does He realize we're waiting
For His healing touch
To make our dreams come true?

There is a one-way window
From His office to the waiting room,
The kind of glass where He sees us,
But we can't see Him.
And so He watches with love.

Do we wait with gratitude and patience?
Do we fix our gaze on
His wonderful Names on the door:
Dr. Elohim,*
Dr. El Shaddai.**

Do we nudge someone
Next to us,
And point out things He's done already?
Maybe not the answers

To our big needs and dreams,
But little bits of blessings,
In a trail,
Which, if we notice them,
And trace their path,
Find they lead us home to His heart,
To peace.

* *"The Strong Faithful One."*
** *"The All-Sufficient One."*

The Music of Jesus

Jesus, despised and rejected,
Then praised,
Whipped and murdered,
Then raised,
Hated and scorned,
Then loved,
Tested and tried,
Then proved.
Walking, healing, seeing, loving,
Speaking, laughing, moving
To the tune of God's own heart,
In perfect time,
In soothing harmony,
A symphony of Life.

To Wrestle and to Dance

To wrestle and to dance,
Life lived
With effort, and with purpose
Not by chance.
Shouts of victory,
Serenades of praise,
A litany of days.
Wrestling with suffering
And sin,
In the ring called wilderness,
Often weary, wondering
If dancing will begin again.
It does.

The music and the movement
Both by grace,
The dance floor is a desert,
A sacred, shining place.
What is the symphony
Of Life
To which we dance?
It is the rushing, rhythmic, bubbling sound
Of Living Water Springs.*

Written in response to a book by Dr. Victor Shepherd called Seasons of Grace.

* see John 7:38.

You Can, You May, You Will

What can you do?
You're stretched out to the maximum,
You feel some people in your life have none
Of your best interests on their hearts,
But for your part,
There is just one thing you must
Do, that is please God with your trust.

What may you do?
Your strength and peace are drained
By the unceasing conflict, your sore heart is pained
While picturing another day
You have to stay,
But there is only one thing that you must
Do, that is please God with your trust.

What will you do?
When wanting so to flee
From every last responsibility,
Escape to some deserted isle,
Avoid this trial,
Yet there is one thing that you must
Do, that is please God with your trust.

Loved, Me by You

Whole…
Wholly obedient,
Free…
Unconditional surrender,
Me…
Giving my life away,
You…
Giving Your love back, in return,
Loved…
Me, by You.

Can I Ever?

Can I ever say never,
Or ever say always,
Even if things are in my control?
For I'm frail and forgetful,
With faults by the mitt-full,
On the best of my down-on-earth days.

Can I ever say never,
Or ever say always,
Thinking God wants what I think is right?
I must bow to His plan,
Or I'm building on sand,
For the rest of my down-on-earth days.

Can I ever say never,
When I live for forever,
And the only sure "always" is God?
With His promise to keep me,
Redeem and equip me,
For the rest of my down-on-earth days.

Can I ever say never,
Or ever say always,
When I know that His love covers all?
My present, my history,
My future—a mystery,
All God's best for my down-on-earth days.

Identity

A small, fragile baby bird,
Bright-eyed, physically complete,
Except for size and strength
And plumage of its own,
Needs the mother's wings
For warmth, protection, security
And consciousness of being loved.

A small, fragile young woman—me—
Bright-eyed, spiritually complete
Except for size and strength
And plumage of my own,
Needs her Heavenly Father's wings
For warmth, protection, security,
And consciousness of being loved.

Yes and No

"No" is a lovely word
In its place,
A humble response to temptation,
"No" means grace.

"No" is an ugly word
When I say
There is some sacrifice for God
I will not pay.

God is "Yes" in Jesus.
He Who bore
My sin, in shame, on the Cross,
Thorns He wore.

Let my heart resound a "Yes"
In grateful praise.
Jesus' sacrifice for me
Shows God's ways.

Sunstreams

Our cat
Sits still and languid,
Lounging in the liquid gold
Of sunlight spilled.

I watch the rays
Pour over feline fur
And hardwood floor.
Our cat relaxes, stretches,
Squints in the brightness,
Not questioning the rightness
Of this joy.

Let me be like this
With God's love
That streams into my life:
Let me allow His warmth
To calm and soothe
My ruffled thoughts and feelings.

The Boxes

The universe cannot contain
Our God,
So why do we keep trying to put
Our God
In boxes we have made?

These mental boxes,
Shaped by our preconceived
Ideas of how God will work,
Are lined with the padding
Of our tightly woven feelings,
Covered with our thought
That common sense and scripture
Are the same (they're not).

For our God,
Who formed the universe
And flung the stars on velvet sky,
Who made baboons and lilies,
Porcupines and mountain peaks—
This same God is so creative
That He'll work in ways
To bless, and to surprise us,
If we'll let Him…

And sometimes even if we don't.

The Praises of Heaven

Heaven is filled with the glory of God,
And constant praises to His name,
Singing strong and sweet,
Loud and clear,
Calling attention to:
His majesty,
His love,
His mercy,
His justice,
His beauty,
His compassion,
His greatness,
His goodness,
His kindness,
His righteousness,
His wisdom.

Lord, help me to keep
A song in my heart
Of praise to You
At all times,
So that,
If I die without warning,
My heart will not have
To shift gears
To enter the praises of heaven.

God's Dwelling Place

"How lovely is your dwelling place, O Lord Almighty!" (Psalm 84:1 NIV)

"I will put my dwelling place among you… I will walk among you, and be your God, and you will be my people." (Leviticus 26:11,12 NIV)

How lovely is Your dwelling place,
O Lord,
You dwell in me,
And make me loved and lovely,
Like You, no matter what.
How, then, could I ever feel worthless?

Should I not simply bask, unmasked,
In this glorious fact?

How to Impress Jesus

What would it take
To astonish the Lord and Maker
Of the universe?

Stunning beauty of face?
Strong, rippling muscles?
Genius of mind?

No, He is the mighty One,
Mind without measure,
Maker of lightening and breezes and roses.

But He turns His full attention
And delight
To the person who has
Faith.*

*see Matthew 8:5-13.

The Honey Hunt

A heart whose waking thought
Is how to seek more honey
From God's word that day,*
Like money,
Currency for souls
To feast on, and to use to buy up
Wisdom for the marketplace of life,
Where deep affections, good decisions
Made and kept, are beyond price.

The honey hunt, a treasure seeker's task
On which my life depends.
And how the harvester of honey
Needs others on this same quest,
To help with the gathering
Of sweet Truth.

Written in response to an article I read about the honey-hunting people of southern Nepal. It is their livelihood, their life's pursuit, and they depend on each other for help during the harvest.
*see Psalm 19:9-10.

The Voice of Goodness

Daily I listen,
Led and fed
By the Shepherd Who is good,
Whose goodness means
His sacrificial love for the sheep.*

Why would I keep
On listening to the voice of stranger-fraud,
When knowing I can follow, free,
The voice of God?
Sometimes I'm still a stupid lamb
And stray, forgetting Whose I am.
I'm His, the Shepherd good
Who, with His rod and staff
Guides me, and would
With arms of love,
Lift me out of harm's way,
Keep me, from the jaws of wolves,
And clutches of the thief,
And apathetic care of hired help.

The voice of goodness
Gives to us, in tones
So gentle and so strong,
Warnings away from wrong,
Directions to green pastures,
Leading to still waters.**

The voice of goodness restores,
Implores the wayward sheep
To keep
Close by each other,
And the Shepherd.

Hear His voice, and trust -
We must—
Our lives depend on listening.

*see John 10:1-18.
**see Psalm 23.

Potter and Clay

Like a lump of clay,
I am
On the Potter's wheel.*

Helpless and hopeless
Except for the love,
And skill and initiative
Of the Potter
As He molds me,
Making me useful for service.

"Your love, O Lord, endures forever—
Do not abandon the works of your hands."**

*see Isaiah 64:8.
**Psalm 138:8.

Jesus, Remember Me

When I read the story
Of the criminal on a cross
Next to Jesus,
I need not say:
"Poor criminal, making his last desperate plea.
Kind Jesus, allowing the wretch
A place in paradise with Him."*

Me, I'm a wretch, too.
I should be hanging there
For my pride,
For my people-pleasing,
For my quiet, respectable compromises,
For my independence from You,
For my social snobbery,
For my "little" lies.

Instead, You, O Lord,
Hung in humble purity,
And let my filthy sins
Batter your body and soul
To Hell.

Thank You for the fresh loving
Garden of Your Resurrection,
And for Your shining, empty tomb.

And Jesus,
Please, remember me when You come into Your Kingdom.

*see Luke 23:32-43.

Spring

A soft, lovely, green morning.
Across the road,
Behind the farmer's field,
The trees and bushes
Rest patiently beneath the morning haze,
Waiting for the eager sun
To lift their damp cloak,
And warm their growing leaves.

This familiar freshness
Can only come
After the cold, dark winter.
Likewise, those who have
Never known a personal, spiritual winter
Will never wake to find
A spring morning moment
In their hearts.

So, thank You Lord,
For the warmth of Your love,
Which lifts my own morning haze
As I wait.

Multiplied Minutes

The little loaves and fishes
Of our days,
We break, with gratitude and praise,
And give to others,
Who are fed,
With life-sustaining Jesus-bread,*
Fragments gathered, baskets full,
Brokenness leaves extra—more—
And so, we bow before Him
And adore.

*see John 6:5-13.

Carpe Diem

Carpe diem, seize the day,
Do I seize it with my fingers?
Making sure my hands are busy,
Making, mixing, fixing, touching.
Having filled my day this way,
Doubt still lingers.

Carpe diem, seize the day,
Do I seize it with my eyes?
Missing nothing, taking in each scene,
Finding every color, every shape.
Having filled my day this way,
Am I now more smart or wise?

Carpe diem, seize the day,
Do I seize with my head?
Mentally assessing each
New person, place, and thing.
Having filled my day this way,
Will I be in peace or dread?

Carpe diem, seize the day,
Do I seize it with my arms?
Wrapping my whole self around,
Opportunities abound; I want the best.
Having filled my day this way,
Perhaps I've done no good, just harm.

Carpe diem, seize the day,
Do I seize it with my spirit?
Leaning close to God and listening,
Fingers touching others with grace,
Eyes noticing people's needs,
Head thinking with the mind of Christ,
Arms reaching out to help and hold.

Having filled my day this way,
Will my Saviour say,
"Well done"?

Integrated Whole

Days and minutes and hours
So fleeting,
Meals and laundry and laughter
Meeting,
In a seamless whole.

Christ's robe on Calvary was seamless, too,
Bargained for by casting lots.
His robe of righteousness
Around me too,
Is without seam,
An integrated whole,
Not mine by chance or dice,
But purchased
By blood and sacrifice.

The Gift of Time

Time management means
More than dancing 'round the clock,
Circling like a hawk
To pounce
Upon an extra minute:
Grab it and go.

Like a page to be read,
The purpose of a person's life
Is hard to decipher,
If there are no margins,
No empty spaces.

Empty is not an enemy;
Constant, frantic, frazzled
Unassessed activity will steal
Away the depth of our relationships.

Cramming more in,
Means less of You and me,
And them.

Dear God,
Time is a gift from You.
Keep me from the trap
Of filling my time,
And draining my soul.

Order

Today I cleaned my sewing box.
The odds and ends
Of tangled threads,
And bits of dust—
I must be daft,
To take delight in such a task,
I ask: Am I just crazy
To rejoice and bask
In such a little job?

Oh, I'm just glad
To see one small part of my life
In order.

Hand-Me-Down Riches

She was the youngest of five children,
In a loving family,
She wore their well-used clothing,
Brand new clothes, a scarcity.

When this household was too noisy
For this youngest of the flock,
Jane would go to see her grandma,
Who lived just around the block.

Her grandma always listened,
Even when it was a whine,
Like: "I want some brand new clothing,
That I can call just mine."

The curtain-filtered sunlight
On her grandma's poster bed,
Made a pattern on her wrinkled cheeks,
As she gently smiled and said:

"Even if you got a new dress,
And coat right from the store,
When you used them every day,
They would not be new, anymore.

But remember all the fun times,
That your family has had,

When you have these in your memory bank,
There's reason to be glad.

For the memory of the laughter
And your parents' words so wise,
Will be with you always new,
Give you strength from family ties."

Jane was quiet as she listened,
To her grandma's loving talk,
She pulled on her sister's sweater,
As she glanced up at the clock.

"It's time I headed home for supper,"
Jane bent down to say good-bye,
"I am going home for memories—
And my favorite cherry pie."

Pieces of Forever

The skyline of her little world,
Is children's forts and blocks,
And the social life she dances,
Is the baby that she rocks.

Small pieces of forever
Are the fragments of her days:
A hug, a kiss, a loving word,
In a child's life, it pays.

Not in stocks and bonds like Wall Street,
Not in costly business clothes,
But investing in a child's heart.
Only a mother knows

Just how raising up a child,
Is the biggest of all tasks,
And disguised as mere mundane
She sees through this earthly mask,

To the fragments of forever,
Passing on her values, true,
Teacher of what really matters,
There is so much left to do.

The skyline of her little world,
Is children's forts and blocks,

And the social life she dances,
Is the baby that she rocks.

And someday, that baby will rock the world
With love.

I Came to Love Him Late*

If only Jesus would come soon.
The thought whirls round
As water from
My brother's bedclothes swirls,
And hope drains down
In blood-stained rivulets
On earth so dry and brown.

The life of my dear Lazarus**
Is slipping from my grip.
I bite my lip.
So hard I try
To tend his wounds,
And keep him clean.
I lean my aching head
On cool clay bricks,
Exhale a prayer:
"Dear God, I cannot fix
My brother anymore."

My hands are raw
From washing long and hard,
Nothing can guard
My nostrils from the stench
Of sores.

If only Jesus would come soon.
It is my waking thought.
It gnaws as daylight dawns.

I pause at sunrise,
Dizzy from fatigue, and think
For one brief, shining moment
That I see Him coming
Down the road.

My load of laundry
Drops like lead.
My head spins round with glee,
And then I sink in misery.
Reality disperses my mirage of Him.

If only Jesus would come soon.
It is a desperate song I sing that has no tune.
We sent for Him.
We wait,
While Lazarus clings feebly
To his last weak thread of life.

If only Jesus would come soon.
I grasp my brother's bony hand,
And make my tears a prayer.
The shawl of midnight air
Has slipped around my shoulders.
Others sleep, I tend the sick one,
Seeking God's own revelation.

If only Jesus came on time,
I say in full despair.
My former litany of hope.
Is now unanswered prayer.

Lazarus lies cold,
In stone entombed,
Wrapped neatly one last time
To rest.

If only Jesus came on time,
We'd sit together:
I would choose the best,
Feast and laugh and listen,
Whether work would beckon me
Or not, I'd listen.

For I came to love Him late.
I used to hate my sister Mary,
Sitting at His feet,***
While I would serve the guests,
You know the rest—
How Christ rebuked
My anxious, scattered frame of mind,
My critical refusal to be kind
To Mary, who had come
To love Him early.

Surely I could learn from her example,
Giving ample space of time and heart
To hear Him and to start
To follow.
How it pains me now to state,
That I came to love Him late.

In matters of responsibility,
To fail in cooking and in cleaning
Would have stripped me

Of my meaning.
I was always organized:
I prized the doing.

Being diligent and dutiful,
The beautiful creation of a flower,
Or a smile
Just escaped me all the while,
As I rushed headlong.
How wrong
To miss the essence of it all.

'Til now,
I bow in joy,
For Jesus came on time
To raise my brother from the dead.

There is no other,
Who makes life where death has been.
No eye has seen
A God like this.
To think I might have missed
The glory of this story.

Most astonishing of all,
Is that I heard my master's call,
And I finally came to love Him,
Just beyond our garden gate,
When He came to help us "late."

*Years ago, Joyce Landorf wrote a book about Martha called I Came to
Love You Late.
**see John 11:1-44.
***see Luke 10:38-42.